PENELOPE HENRY

at the Circus

PENELOPE HENRY

at the Circus

Kathleen W. Forbes

ISBN: 978-1-4866-0793-8

Printed in Canada

Word Alive Press
131 Cordite Road, Winnipeg, MB R3W 1S1
www.wordalivepress.ca

WORD ALIVE
—— P R E S S ——

MIX
Paper from
responsible sources
FSC® C016245
FSC
www.fsc.org

Library and Archives Canada Cataloguing in Publication

Forbes, Kathleen W., 1930-, author
        Penelope Henry at the circus / Kathleen W. Forbes.

Issued in print and electronic formats.
ISBN 978-1-4866-0793-8 (pbk.).--ISBN 978-1-4866-0794-5 (pdf).--
ISBN 978-1-4866-0795-2 (html).--ISBN 978-1-4866-0796-9 (epub)

        I. Title.

PS8611.O7215P46 2016   jC813'.6   C2015-901540-5
                                            C2015-901541-3

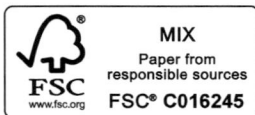

CONTENTS

1.	Runaway Monkey	1
2.	Showtime	15
3.	Dinty to the Rescue	35
4.	Thrills, Chills, and Goosebumps	42
5.	Get Me Out of Here	59
6.	Happy Birthday, Penny	69
7.	Skulduggery	78
8.	Sweet Dreams	92

CHAPTER 1

RUNAWAY MONKEY

"Hurry, hurry, Jillybean!" Penny pounded on her best friend's door. "We're going to be late for the parade. We want to get a good spot so we can see."

She looked up when a window was thrown open upstairs and Jillybean poked her head out.

"What's all the fuss?" Jillybean asked. "You'll wake my papa! He's working night shift and just got to sleep."

Penny tried to lower her voice. "But seriously, the circus parade starts in thirty minutes."

"I'm ready. I'll be down in a couple of minutes."

The window closed with a bang and Penny hopped impatiently up and down 'til Jillybean appeared at the front door. "Just a minute!" Jillybean checked one pocket, then the other. "Oh, good! I do have my jellybeans." She never went anywhere without her jellybeans. That's why Penny had given her the nickname.

"Is Mandy ready?" Penny asked.

"Mandy left about an hour ago with Mama."

Jillybean's sister Mandy was also her twin. Even though they looked exactly alike, they were not alike in other ways. Mandy was very quiet and shy and Jillybean was very much like Penny, ready for any adventure, and Penny and Jillybean usually found more than their share of adventure and scary situations.

Suddenly, they heard a loud whooping and hollering as Barney Brindle ran past like a streak of lightning with a small monkey sitting on his shoulders. The monkey had one hairy arm wrapped around Barney's neck and a tiny furry hand clamped over the boy's right eye. Barney's other eye blinked wildly as he streaked around the two girls in circles. Barney tried without success to knock the monkey off his shoulders while Penny's pet magpie, Blackie, swooped and shrieked excitedly around them.

"Get it off me!" Barney yelled. "Help me, Penny! Please... please... Penny!"

Tears streamed down his face and his arms flailed wildly while Blackie squawked in a continuous, aggravating chatter: "Help me, Penny! Help me, Penny!"

Penny and Jillybean started running alongside Barney.

"What can we do?" Penny asked.

"I don't know," he cried. "Just do something!"

"Stop running in circles and I'll try!" Penny smiled to herself. "It's a good thing I made Frisky stay home, or he would have been running circles with you and barking up a storm. I didn't want him chasing the animals in the parade."

The girls couldn't control their giggles, which didn't make Barney feel any better. Penny quickly pulled her jacket off, and after a couple of tries she managed to throw it over Barney's head, covering both him and the monkey.

"Yikes, now I can't see!" Barney screamed as he fell onto the road.

Penny and Jillybean pounced on him and they each made a grab for the monkey, which was now wrapped in the jacket and also unable to see. It let go of Barney's head and tried to struggle out of the jacket, but Penny held on tight until Barney was able to free himself.

"Whew! That was scary!" he croaked, clawing at his neck. "I didn't even know what it was that had a hold of me. Thanks, Penny! That was pretty quick thinking with the jacket. I don't know what I would have done if you and Jill hadn't been here."

Penny and Jillybean were still laughing. "Where did he come from?" Penny asked as the monkey's frightened little face peeked out of the folds of the jacket. "Oh no you don't, you little rascal." She wrapped her captive tightly. "You're not getting away 'til we find your owner."

"He must have escaped from the circus," Barney said. "I was walking to the parade grounds when he jumped out of a tree and landed on my head. I didn't see him coming and I thought I'd die of fright. But he doesn't look too scary now, does he?"

"Oh, I think he's really cute. It's okay, little guy," Penny said softly as she stroked the monkey's head. "We're not going to hurt you." The animal stopped struggling.

Jillybean reached into her pocket and popped her favourite candy, a green jellybean, into the monkey's mouth. The girls giggled with delight as they watched him make funny faces trying to chew the sticky candy. Barney was fascinated but didn't want to get too close after the fright he'd had.

"We must find your owner, little one," Penny said, cuddling the monkey close. "You must be really scared. But we need to hurry or we'll miss the parade. Let's go, guys!"

They arrived at the grounds just as the parade was starting.

"Over here, Penny! We saved a place for you!" a voice called.

"Oh! Look, Jillybean, there's Summer and Wolf with their parents!" Penny exclaimed with delight.

They ran to the other side of the parade route to join their friends. Penny's brother Zinger had already found Wolf and they were squeezed right into the front of the line.

Penny's parents were delighted to see Summer and Wolf's parents again. They had all enjoyed a wonderful holiday together at the campground at Blueberry Mountain a couple of months before. What a wonderful adventure it had been!

"We thought you weren't coming," Summer said. "The parade has started." Suddenly, she saw the jacket move. "What have you got there? Is it a puppy?"

"No," Penny giggled. "It's a monkey!"

"A monkey?" Summer was startled. "Where did you get him?"

Penny explained what had happened and introduced Barney to her friends. "Barney was the one who actually found him, and now we have to find the owner."

"The circus lost a monkey," Summer told them. "They were asking over the sound system if anyone had seen a small monkey to please come to the big tent and ask for the ringmaster. There is a reward for him. Oh look!" She pointed. "The clowns are coming."

"I'll wait until after the parade," Penny decided. "Then I'll take our little runaway to the tent."

The clowns cavorted, chased each other, and rolled down the track. They did somersaults, handsprings, and all kinds of acrobatics. One clown was on a unicycle, and he had a monkey riding on his head to the delight of the crowd. Penny and Jillybean laughed along with the crowd, but they pointed gleefully at Barney.

"This little guy must have been practicing on you, Barney," Penny joked. The kids all got a kick out of Barney's red-faced discomfort. "He thought you were a clown!"

"That's not funny," Barney grumbled.

"Oh look, Penny!" Jillybean pointed to a baby elephant which kept running away from his mother as she gently swatted him back in line with her trunk.

"He's adorable," Penny whispered softly.

The seals and lions rumbled by in their rolling cages and the decorated and ribboned Arabian horses pranced by, their brushed manes and tails fanning and swishing. The trick riders somersaulted from one side to the other as the band played the old marches. These were followed by gaily decorated floats of all colours, displaying trapeze artists swinging and flying just enough to make everyone want to come to the show to see more.

The parade lasted for about thirty minutes, then suddenly it was over. The excited crowd started to move along.

"We'd better take our little monkey friend to the tent," Penny said. "Let's go before he manages to wriggle out of my jacket and get lost again."

They arrived at the big tent just as a very tall, very elegant man was coming out of the main entrance. He wore a red velvet jacket, black breeches, a white shirt with fancy ruffles down the front, as well as high black boots and a tall black top hat.

"What are you doing here, kids?" he asked. "The show doesn't start until two o'clock."

"Are you the ringmaster, sir?" Penny inquired.

"I am," he said. "What can I do for you?"

"My name is Penny Henry, sir, and we found a little monkey!"

"You did? Well, where is he and how did you get him?" the ringmaster asked.

"He's in my jacket." Penny opened the jacket and the monkey leaped into the ringmaster's arms.

"There you are, you daffy little simian," he chuckled. "Been off on another adventure, have you? Tommy was quite upset when you disappeared."

Penny told the man how they came to have the monkey and what a time they'd had getting him off Barney's head.

The ringmaster roared with laughter. "Wish I'd seen that! His name is Gypsy. A good name for the little scamp, don't you think? That's the third time this week he's wandered off on his own. I guess he likes the trees here. Well, I promised a reward." He reached into his pocket for his wallet.

"Oh, we don't want a reward, sir," Penny told him. "We're just glad we found his owner."

"Is that so? Well, well, now. That's unusual! My name is Mr. Daniel Ferguson and I own this circus. If you don't want a reward, then we must do something nice for you. Gypsy belongs to my son, Tommy, and he'll be very happy to have him back. So how would you like to have free tickets for this afternoon's show? Would a dozen tickets be enough for you and your families, do you think? Front row seats?"

The children's beaming faces revealed how thrilled they were. "Oh thank you, sir!" Penny gushed.

"Hey, Billy!" Mr. Ferguson shouted to a man inside the door. "Bring me a dozen tickets! Front row seats!"

"Right you are, Mr. Ferguson." Billy ducked into the tent and was back again immediately.

"There you go, kids." Mr. Ferguson gave the tickets to Penny. "I'll leave it up to you, my dear, to pass them around. And how would you like Tommy to take you on a tour of the circus and the animals tomorrow morning? You can see how they're cared for, and meet the performers."

"Oh, thank you," Penny said. "We would love to."

"I'll arrange for Tommy to meet you after the show to set it up. So don't be late, Miss Henry!"

"We won't, sir!" the kids all replied at once.

"Wow! This is great!" Barney exclaimed. "Your monkey can ride on my shoulders any time, mister."

"Better not let him hear you say that, or he just might take you up on it," Mr. Ferguson said, laughing. "See you later at the show!"

"Yes, sir," said Penny. "We'll be there with bells on. And thank you very much."

Penny gave each of them a ticket. "Let's go find Zinger and Wolf and Mandy. That will leave us with five. If we give one to each of our parents and Mandy, we'll be three short."

"Well, my mom and dad won't be able to go," said Barney. "Their bakery is open this afternoon."

"And my papa won't be able to go either," said Jillybean. "He's working nights and will be sleeping. But Mama will come."

"Perfect then," Penny told them. "We'll have enough."

Blackie swooped down to see why everyone was so happy and landed on Penny's shoulder. Summer tickled him on the neck and he nuzzled his beak into her hand. Everybody loved Blackie because he talked a blue streak and kept them entertained.

"Hi there, Blackie," Summer whispered. "I'm glad to see you again. We missed you a lot."

"Have you seen Dinty?" Penny asked.

"No," Summer answered. "But he's still helping kids. My cousin, Beaver, who's only five years old, climbed a tree and was scared to come down. He wouldn't come down for me or Wolfie, but Dinty heard him crying, and he jumped into the tree with one leap and helped him down. Beaver stopped crying as soon as Dinty showed up. He always shows up in time.

"I wish I could see him again," said Penny. "But he did say he would come if we needed him, didn't he?"

"Yes, he did," Summer agreed. "And he always keeps his promises to little kids. He's a very nice leprechaun."

"Does he ever leave the campground?" Jillybean asked.

"I don't know, but he would if you were in trouble. He'd be here in a flash."

Barney was looking at the girls like they were crazy, but he didn't want to say anything since they had just saved his life. How many times in a guy's life would he have a monkey jump out of a tree and ride on his head? Barney was sure the girls had saved him from a fate worse than death. But a leprechaun? Ridiculous!

"Well, let's go and give the tickets to our parents," Penny suggested. "After lunch, it will be time to go to the show. Mr. Ferguson told us not to be late, so I think we should get there by one-thirty."

They found everyone's parents with Mandy, Zinger, and Wolf at the lemonade and hotdog stand. Miss Sprightly, Penny's teacher, was talking to them about Penny's upcoming birthday party, planned for the following day. She was invited, along with Penny's whole class.

"There you are!" Penny's mama greeted them. "Come and get a hotdog or a hamburger if you prefer. We'd like four more lemonades," she told the man. "All right, tell the man what you would like. You too, Barney!"

"Oh, thank you, Mrs. Henry," Barney said. "I'd like a hotdog, if that's okay."

"That's great, Barney. All right now, hands up for hotdogs," Mama said. She turned to the man in the booth. "Looks like they're all having hotdogs."

While the kids helped themselves to ketchup and mustard, they told their parents all about the little monkey and that everybody had been invited to the show.

"Front row seats?" Mr. Henry exclaimed. "I don't know how you do it, but you always seem to get in on these terrific deals, Penny."

They had a good laugh over Barney's run-in with the monkey and poor Barney blushed bright red.

Penny introduced Barney to Summer's parents, Storm Cloud and Autumn. Most people called her dad Stormy. Penny then filled Barney in on some of the adventures they'd had at the campground at Blueberry Mountain. A nervous shiver revealed that Barney was spooked by the tales.

"I wish I'd been there," he said. "We never have good stories like that when we go camping with the Boy Scouts."

Mandy and the two younger boys stayed with their parents, but Barney decided to hang out with the three girls until it was time to leave for the show. He wanted to hear more about their last trip together and decided he didn't want to lose out on whatever adventures would surely crop up if he stuck with Penny. Her father was right! She did seem to attract strange and interesting adventures. Any time there was a disaster or something out of the ordinary in the town of Green Oaks, Penny seemed to have caused it, or she was right in the middle of it. Yeah! For sure, Barney would stick with the girls.

CHAPTER 2

SHOWTiME

The big tent was packed to the door. People were still trying to get in, but they were told to come back for the evening show. They had come from miles around to be entertained in the big top, a splendid, colossal tent that boasted two separate rings to keep two continuous performances going on at the same time.

Penny and her friends and family were all in their front row seats.

"I can't believe how lucky we are to have these seats," said Penny.

"Me too," said a familiar voice from the vicinity of Penny's left elbow. "Move your arm, Penny lass. The arm of the chair is just big enough for me."

"Who…what on earth? Is that you, Dinty?" she asked. "I can't see you!"

"That's the idea," Dinty replied. "My wee family and I don't have money to buy tickets."

"You mean, your family is here too?"

"Of course they are. Do you think we'd miss a big circus like this? They're scattered around the tent wherever they can find a place to sit, without being stepped on or sat on. They're invisible, of course."

"Of course," Penny agreed. She still couldn't help looking around to see if she could see any of Dinty's family.

"Who are you talking to, Penny?" Summer asked.

"Who do you think? Dinty Finnigan, of course!"

"Of course!" Summer nodded her head. "He must have caught a ride with us when we drove to town. Hi there, Dinty!"

Zinger's and Wolf's heads snapped around when they heard Summer.

"Dinty's here?" Zinger asked. "Where is he?"

"Shush, Zinger. He's sitting on my chair arm." Penny told him. "Don't draw attention to him."

"How could I do that?" said Zinger. "He's invisible!"

Dinty chuckled. "Smart boy!"

"Are you telling me there's a little man sitting on your chair arm, Penny?" Barney said out of the side of his mouth as he squinted sideways in Penny's direction.

"Who's your friend, Penny?" Dinty asked.

"Oh, that's just Barney. He's okay! He knows all about you."

"Does he now? Does he always talk like a gangster out of the side of his mouth?"

Barney heard him and his head snapped around.

"No, sir! I'm sorry, sir." Barney's eyes darted back and forth. "I can't see you, sir."

"Och, now! Did you hear that, Penny? He called me sir." Dinty was highly amused. "You'll see me if you need me, young fellow."

"I sure needed you today," said Barney.

"Oh, you mean when the monkey took a shine to you? You didn't need me then. Penny and Jill did just fine."

"You mean you saw that?" Penny asked him.

"Of course I did! I told you I'd keep an eye on you. Barney just happened along and I enjoyed the fun. I haven't laughed so much in a long time."

"It wasn't funny to me," Barney grumbled.

The word had gotten along to the rest of the group that Dinty was here and they were getting a little noisy, so Dinty told them they'd better be quiet or they would get thrown out before the show started.

Just then, a chorus of bugles sounded and the band started up. The curtains parted at the entrance to the arena, and suddenly Mr. Ferguson, the ringmaster, appeared. The bugles introduced him with a musical fanfare and the crowd became very quiet.

"Ladies and gentlemen and children of all ages, allow me to present to you the Ferguson Family Circus. We will take you to a world of fantasy, to visit exotic animals from faraway lands, performing dogs, seals, lions, bears, monkeys, and elephants, and we will entertain you with the very best athletes in acrobatics, trapeze, and horsemanship. We'll also have a touch of magic. So make yourselves comfortable and prepare to enjoy yourselves. Let the show begin!"

The drums rolled and the cymbals clanged. With another loud fanfare from the bugles and saxes, a line of animals began to parade around the ring, led by the beautiful white Arabian horses and their delightful equestrian riders arrayed in white and silver. The riders stood on the horses' backs with their arms outstretched, looking just like angels. There was an awestruck "Ooooh…" from the crowd.

Next came the little dogs and their trainers. The dogs danced and tumbled and followed their trainer. Their antics delighted the crowd. Then the lions slinked along, looking very fierce. Their trainers stayed close and in command, and everyone remained quiet until they passed.

The seals, bears, and other animals followed, and the monkeys got into all kinds of mischief with the clowns. The acrobats cartwheeled and back-flipped around the ring, followed by elephants, unicycles, and many other attractions. Then they all disappeared behind the curtains and Mr. Ferguson came out to introduce the first act.

"May I present to you, all the way from Paris, France, six-time world champion trapeze artists, the Framboise family."

The crowd became very quiet as the catcher grabbed his swing and left his platform at the opposite side. He began to swing back and forth. He flipped upside-down and waited. A young man reached for his swing and swung back and forth. Suddenly, he left the swing in mid-air and somersaulted over and over three times. The crowd gasped, thinking he might fall, but the catcher caught him firmly and held him while he swung back towards the platform. Just before he reached the other side, the trapeze artist double-somersaulted and landed solidly on his two feet on the platform. The audience oohed and ahhed, delighting in the thrill of the risk.

Then it was the young lady's turn. She slid onto the swing, pulled herself up, bent over, and grasped the seat with her hands. Kicking her feet into the air, she executed a handstand while swinging back and forth.

Suddenly, she left the swing in mid-air and twisted around to execute two backflips before the catcher caught her by the ankles. The crowd was horrified. They held their breath to see how she would manage to get herself right-side up. But they shouldn't have worried, because she left the catcher in mid-air again and did one and a half somersaults before grasping her swing and landing safely on the far platform. There was a loud whoosh as the audience blew air out between their teeth in relief.

The ringmaster spoke in a hushed voice. "And now, ladies and gentlemen, the youngest member of the Framboise family, Jason, who is only ten years old, will attempt a double twist and backflip, and on the return he will execute a single twist and a triple somersault. We ask that you be very quiet as this young man performs these difficult moves for someone of his tender age."

The audience held its breath. Jason looked very small on the high platform. The catcher sent the swing over and he grabbed on. It was thrilling to watch him. He was as agile as a monkey, and his small body executed the difficult moves like a veteran performer. He hurled himself through the air like a rubber ball, twisting and turning and flipping with precision. He was without fear!

"Ooooh! Ahhhh!" the crowd whispered in awe. When he arrived safely back on the platform, the audience went wild. They jumped up, screaming and cheering, and shouted, "Bravo! Bravo! Bravo!"

Jason bowed. Then the three performers swung out on their swings and somersaulted back and forth, passing each other in mid-air. The catcher was a very busy man while this was going on.

Penny and her friends were caught up in the magic and Dinty was heard shouting, "Good show, lad! Good show! Bravo!"

When the performance was over, the audience gave them a standing ovation to show their appreciation.

"And now ladies and gentlemen, all the way from India, Mahmoud and the largest living land animals in the world, the wondrous, majestic elephants. You will see how graceful these animals are and respect their intelligence as they perform for you."

The baby elephant poked its trunk through the curtains. Its mama gave a gentle push with her trunk and the baby staggered out into the arena. The children were delighted. Three more of the gigantic beasts lumbered forward and a small man in a turban and red-and-white satin suit ran forward. This had to be Mahmoud!

Raising his stick, Mahmoud gave a command and the elephants formed a straight line. He tapped his stick on a barrel and the elephants raised their front legs as though they were begging. The crowd loved them. The mama elephant pushed her baby with her trunk to make it sit up, but with no success. Baby just snuggled its mama, as all babies do. The mama elephant picked up baby with her trunk and swung it back and forth like she was rocking a cradle while the band played a lullaby. Everybody laughed and applauded, and the elephants trumpeted.

Next, they stood on their front legs, with their back legs up in the air. When they came down, Mahmoud tapped his cane again and they did a right turn and stood one behind the other. Now the mama elephant put the baby down and pushed it behind her with her trunk. The elephants all stood on their hind legs and placed one front foot on the shoulder of the elephant in front. The baby placed its trunk on its mama's hind leg as high as he could reach. He was so adorable, and the audience loved him.

"Ladies and gentlemen. My son, Tommy, will now select a young lady from the audience to be part of the next act."

A small figure in a blue satin suit ran across the arena and stood right in front of Penny. He reached out his hand to her and bowed.

"My name is Tommy Ferguson. Will you do me the honour of being my partner on a ride you will never forget? Don't worry! There is nothing to fear, and I will show you what to do."

Penny glanced sideways at her papa, expecting him to say no, but he was grinning from ear to ear. "Go ahead, Penny. You'll have fun!" he told her. "You will take good care of her, won't you, young man?"

"Yes, sir!" Tommy told him.

Penny followed him to the centre ring, wondering what on earth she would have to do. The elephants were so humongous, she was afraid to get too close.

"Penny, this is Paquin," Tommy said. "She is very gentle. Sit here on her trunk right next to me, and I will ride up with you, and then we will walk on her shoulders. You will sit in a nice comfortable saddle and hold on to the harness. Are you ready?"

"Oh, I couldn't do that, Tommy. What if I fall?"

"There's nothing to be afraid of. I'll be with you until you are safely in the saddle. Okay! Shall we go?"

Tommy climbed onto the elephant's trunk and reached out his hand to Penny.

Penny decided to go for it.

"Right here, missy!" Mahmoud said, reaching for her other hand. "I'll help you!"

Penny sat down gingerly and Tommy held her with one arm around her waist.

"Up, Paquin," he said, and suddenly they were soaring high into the air. It was like being on a Ferris wheel. Soon Paquin's trunk was on a level with her shoulders. Tommy stood up and reached for Penny's hand to help her. "Okay, Penny. You can stand up now! Paquin's trunk is wide and I won't let you fall. That's it! Now, just follow me onto Paquin's shoulders. You're doing great! There is your saddle. Hold on to the harness, Penny!"

Penny felt like she was on top of a mountain. The lights were so terribly bright and she couldn't see the audience, but she felt wonderful.

"How do you feel, Penny?" Tommy asked.

"Oh, this is super!"

"Good! Now, I'm going to ride Timber." Tommy told her. "You will follow Mahmoud and I will follow you."

"But I don't know how to guide Paquin," Penny said nervously.

"Don't worry!" Tommy assured her. "Paquin knows what to do. She will follow Cabole and Mahmoud."

With that, he shinnied down Paquin's trunk and ran to Timber. He jumped onto the trunk. Like a flash, he got onto Timber's shoulders, grinning across at Penny.

Mahmoud quickly mounted Cabole by jumping onto his trunk. Up he went, vaulting over Cabole's head and onto his shoulders. He then gave the beast an order and Cabole began walking around one ring, then the other. Paquin followed with Penny, and Tommy brought up the rear. Baby walked beside his mama.

Penny had lots of room on the elephant's shoulders, but she hung on real tight just the same. The band played a marching melody and Mahmoud and Tommy both stood on their elephants' backs. Then they each did a handstand and double backflip, landing on their feet with their arms stretched out wide.

Penny was content just sitting where she was and discovered she was enjoying herself. She was glad that she wasn't expected to do any more than ride.

The elephants paraded back to the centre of the stage and Tommy and Mahmoud slid down their elephants' trunks just like they were on a backyard slide.

"Okay, Penny," Timmy said. "Paquin will kneel down when I tell her to, and then you can slide down her trunk. Don't worry, I'll come up there and help you. Just hang on to the harness until I join you."

"Okay, Tommy." Penny nodded her head. "This is fun! I'm starting to get the hang of it!"

At a signal from Tommy, Paquin knelt down on her front knees, then her back knees, and Tommy ran up the trunk, which Paquin raised to bring him right in front of Penny. He offered her his hand.

"Just follow me!" he said. "Put your arms around my waist. That's good! Off we go!"

With a scary squeal from the horns in the band, they slid to the ground.

"Great job, Penny! Now we must turn around and bow!" Tommy said.

Tommy, Mahmoud, and Penny all bowed, and Mahmoud tapped the elephants on their knees. They bowed too. Baby managed to go down on one knee.

The audience applauded and Penny could hear Zinger and the rest of her friends all shouting her name. She felt like a big star.

"Thank you, Penny," Mr. Ferguson said. "A big hand, ladies and gentlemen, for Mahmoud and his elephants, Timber, Paquin, Cabole, and baby Pia. And a special hand for Tommy and his guest, Miss Penny Henry!"

The crowd whistled and applauded as Tommy escorted Penny back to her seat.

"Thank you, Penny. You were wonderful! I have to go now, but I'll see you all later, after the show. Thanks for finding Gypsy!"

He ran quickly to the curtain and disappeared as the clowns tumbled out.

"It was my head Gypsy jumped on," Barney grumbled. "I should have had the elephant ride." No one was listening.

"Wow, Penny!" Zinger exclaimed. "That was super!"

The others all agreed.

"I was frightened half to death when you were up on that beast," Mama said. "You have no fear, my dear child. Sometimes I think you'll be the end of me. Of course, Grandma used to say the same about me."

"She's a lot like Wolf," said Stormy. "We never know what he's going to get into."

"You're a real pip, Penny lass," Dinty whispered to her. "I thought I'd have to rescue you. But you did real good! I'm proud of you, and that's a fact!"

"Thanks, Dinty! It was super fun!"

Between acts, the clowns played tricks on each other, bursting water balloons and chasing one another with water pistols to the delight of the children. They were marvellous acrobats and one big clown rode a tiny little unicycle while a dwarf rode a bicycle that was six feet tall. The clowns walked on stilts that made them nine feet tall, and tiny little dwarfs tumbled around doing gymnastics.

When the next act was introduced, they all disappeared through the curtain like magic. It only took a few seconds.

"Ladies, gentlemen, and kids, hold on to your seats and be very quiet, because our next act is none other than my elder son, Martin, and my lovely wife, Lynda, with Simba, the fierce king of the jungle and his pride of African lions."

The band played some enchanting African music and a beautiful, slim lady with light blond hair stepped into the ring. She wore a gorgeous pink satin gown, with a matching pink hat over her flowing curls. A young man in a white satin jumpsuit walked over to a hidden door behind the curtain, and with one quick movement he raised the door.

Simba, the biggest, fiercest lion the children had ever seen, furtively entered the ring. It was easy to see that he was the boss. He was slinking along, nose close to the ground, and his family followed closely behind. Their tails swished slowly from side to side and their eyes burned as they focused intently on the two figures in the ring.

"Thank goodness I'm not in this act," Penny said. "I wonder if they've had their dinner."

"Good thinking, Penny m'lass," Dinty agreed. "You might have been lunch."

"Gross!" She drew her breath in between her teeth in a soft whistle. "Oh, look at them jumping through that fiery hoop! I do hope their fur doesn't catch fire. The flames are really high."

"Oh, no! I can't look," Jillybean cried. She threw her arms around Penny and buried her head in Penny's shoulder as one of the lions growled ferociously and swiped its immense paws at the ringmaster's wife. Lynda cracked her whip and demonstrated her control with some quick commands to calm the beast.

"Look, Jillybean! Tommy's mom and brother aren't afraid, and they're making the lions sit on very high stools," Penny said. "When they crack the whips, the lions obey them."

Jill's head swivelled around. Lynda and Martin were certainly in control of the scary animals. Martin even put his head in Simba's mouth. He said he was checking to see if he needed to go to the dentist.

"That would be a *very* brave dentist," shouted Zinger, and everybody around them laughed. Zinger loved the attention and he was on a roll. He had a gleam of mischief in his eyes. "I wonder if the dentist gives Simba a lollypop for being good, or if Simba takes a bite out of the dentist instead." He screwed up his face as he thought about it.

"The kid's a comedian," a man behind them grumbled. "Better be quiet, kid, or they'll make you part of the act."

Papa glared at the guy and told him to leave his son alone. The man's reply was drowned out by the applause for the act. Lynda and Martin were taking their bows.

As they left the rings, the trick riders swept out into the arena. Tommy and Jason were riding beautiful white Arabian horses, displaying their equestrian skills as they jumped over high hurdles. Around the outside of the rings, talented riders went through their routines.

Suddenly, Penny noticed a tiny little figure toddling out into the arena.

"Dinty!" she cried. "That's little Mikey Rumble!"

CHAPTER 3

DINTY TO THE RESCUE

"I'm way ahead of you," Dinty cried, and with a whoosh, he was gone.

Mikey seemed to rise up in the air all by himself and landed on Tommy's horse.

"Hello, Tommy, m'lad," Dinty greeted him. "I hope you don't mind a couple of hitchhikers."

"Wh—what's happened?" Tommy asked. "And who are you?"

Dinty had made himself visible to him, but not to the crowd. The crowd thought a miracle had just happened and they were on their feet cheering Tommy for his bravery in rescuing Mikey.

"Dinty Finnigan's m' name. Rescuing kids is m' game. Wave to the crowd, Tommy. You're their hero!"

"But I'm not a hero," Tommy said. "You are! How did you do that? You're only half the size of me! Are you one of the dwarfs? I've never seen you before!"

"No, I'm not one of the seven dwarfs," said Dinty. "But I am one of the little people. I'm a leprechaun. You can see me, but the crowd can't, except for Penny and Zinger, that is. Now finish this round while I hold wee Mikey. Don't worry! I'm stronger than I look."

Tommy signalled to Jason. "I think we'd better escort young Mikey back to his mother. Look at her!"

It was easy to spot Mikey's mother. She had climbed through the ropes, hanging on to them like she was going to faint. Her moans now changed to cries of joy as she saw her son riding towards her.

"Mama!" Mikey shouted with glee. "Nice horsey, Mama!"

"Oh bless you," she managed to gasp. "I don't know how you did that or how I can thank you. I didn't see him slip under the ropes."

"Mikey's okay, ma'am," Tommy consoled her. "He's had a bit of an adventure. Bye, Mikey! Stay with your mama now. You hear?"

"I won't let him out of my sight from now on," his mama said. "Thank you again, young man."

"You're welcome, ma'am. Okay, Jason. Let's go!"

The two boys and their horses seemed to fly around the arena, and the crowd rose to their feet, cheering and giving them a standing ovation.

"Well, that was a wee bit of excitement," Dinty whispered to Penny. "The lad had the time of his life, but I'm not sure his mama will get over it, at least not for a while."

"You were super, Dinty," Penny told him. "Nobody is going to believe what they saw. It looked like Mikey jumped up on that horse all by himself."

Dinty laughed. "Yes. I'd like to hear the stories they'll tell. They'll probably think it was magic."

"Well, it was magic! Wasn't it?" Penny said, pointing to the curtain. "Oh look, everybody! The bears are coming and they're dressed in clothes." She laughed as the mama bear chased her wandering baby and pushed him into the ring.

A beautiful girl with golden curls and a blue frilly dress walked into the arena.

"Allow me to introduce you to my daughter Jenny, folks," Mr. Ferguson's voice boomed over the mike. "She's going to entertain you with her dancing bears."

The band played a marching melody and Jenny marched around the ring, the bears following in formation and keeping perfect time to the music. The great, lumbering beasts were quite graceful as they stepped carefully behind Jenny. Baby wandered a bit, but his mama kept pushing him back into line.

Jenny put her hand up to order them to stop, and they obediently marched in place. Then she put her right arm out and the bears all turned to face the audience. Suddenly, the band switched to a waltz, and Jenny raised her hand. Her little dancing troupe reared up on their hind legs. Jenny swayed from side to side in time to the music while the bears followed her lead and swayed along with her. The children clapped and cheered with delight.

Jenny moved in front of the papa bear and swayed with him. The audience swayed along. Then Jenny turned slowly to the tempo and the huge bear followed her. Next it was mama bear's turn; she moved gracefully as she followed Jenny's lead. Baby bear just started spinning in place. He was so adorable!

The children cheered as Jenny led the little troupe into another marching melody. This time, they marched twelve steps in one direction, then twelve steps in the other, and repeated this formation several times. Jenny raised both her hands and gave the signal to stop, and the bears turned again to face the audience.

The music ended with a flourish and Jenny bowed. She pointed to papa bear and gave the signal to bow, which he did. Mama bear bowed next, and baby bear just snuggled against mama as the crowd applauded. The band played another march and Jenny led her troupe of dancers through the curtains. The audience applauded and cheered as Jenny came out and bowed again, three more times. Then she ran nimbly back through the forest of curtains.

The lights came on, announcing intermission, and everyone took a break to buy popcorn and pop.

"Wasn't that super?" Penny exclaimed.

"Sure was!" shouted Zinger. "I didn't know bears could dance."

Dinty could be heard chuckling to himself. "Well, I'd better check on my wee ones," he said. "I hope they're behaving themselves."

Penny could hear the tiny voices from somewhere overhead. "Hi, daddy! We're up here."

"There you are, you wee rascals!" Dinty waved at them. "That's a good place for you. You won't get stepped on up there!"

"I can't see them," Penny said. "Where are they?"

"Just above us, on the catwalk. If you look this side of the pole, you'll see them. They're with their mama."

Penny spotted Blackie and smiled to herself.

"I see Blackie got in," she said to Dinty. "It's amazing... I didn't hear him mimicking any of the performers. He's usually very noisy."

"Yes, he was pretty quiet for a change, wasn't he? Well, my wee family is to the right of him."

Penny looked to where Dinty was pointing, and there they were! Three little elves who looked just like Dinty. They were sitting with a lady leprechaun, and they were all waving. Penny waved back as they ducked behind the pole.

"They're a wee bit shy," Dinty told her. "They're not used to people being able to see them."

"I hope I didn't frighten them," Penny said.

"Oh, I don't think so. They've seen you before."

"Who are you waving at, Penny?" Zinger asked.

Penny didn't want to draw Zinger's attention to Dinty's family, so she pointed to Blackie, perched on the ropes.

"Blackie's up there!" she said. "See! On the ropes! He has a good view, don't you think?"

"Sure does," Zinger agreed. "Wish I could get up there, but I can't fly."

"Good girl, Penny," said Dinty. "You managed to divert Zinger's attention to Blackie."

"But why can I see them and Zinger can't?" Penny asked.

"Because Zinger would make too much fuss, and I don't want to scare them off. They're fine where they are. Don't worry! I'll arrange it so the other kids will see them before we go home to the campground."

CHAPTER 4

THRiLLS, CHiLLS, AND *GOOSEBUMPS*

The jangling and clanging of cymbals and the blaring of bugles and trumpets announced that the second half of the show was about to begin. As before, the clowns, monkeys, and riders made a sweep of the arena, performing their tumbling acts and tricks to get the crowd warmed up.

Everyone settled back into their seats and enjoyed the antics of the clowns and monkeys. Tommy's little monkey, Gypsy, rode on his shoulders. Gypsy kissed him on the cheek and crawled up his face onto his head, to the delight of the crowd. It didn't seem to bother Tommy at all. He grinned as he stood on the horse's back, skipping rope. The monkey hung on with both little hands wrapped around his head. Barney laughed louder than anybody.

Just as quickly as the performers had appeared, they were gone, disappearing through the curtains.

"Ladies, gentlemen, and children," Mr. Ferguson said in a hushed voice. "I am going to ask you to be very quiet, because the next act requires great skill and steady nerves. Voltare the Great will perform his knife-throwing act while his partner, the beautiful Della Marie, is strapped to that spinning wheel."

"Oh no!" Penny whispered. "I can't look."

Jillybean and Mandy buried their heads in their hands, but they peeked out between their fingers. Zinger and Wolf's eyes grew big as saucers, but they weren't about to miss any of it. Summer just looked scared.

"It will be fine, Penny," Dinty whispered. "Voltare never makes a mistake."

"Do you know him?" she whispered in awe.

"For many years," he told her. "Hush now. You just be quiet."

Voltare was dressed in slim black pants, with a black vest and white shirt. He wore a black sombrero and looked very smart. Miss Della Marie wore a beautiful white satin gown with a red sash around her waist. Voltare's assistant strapped her onto the wheel, then grabbed the handle and gave it a spin.

Voltare lined up the knives in this hand like a fan. Della Marie was spinning really fast as Voltare chose a knife and threw it with lightning speed. It struck the board just above

Della Marie's head. The audience gasped and held their breath. Then he threw five knives so fast that they looked like a blur. They landed between each finger of her right hand, and one landed so close to the right side of her face that Penny would have thought she would blink. He then threw five more knives, one between each of the fingers of her left hand, and another just left of her face.

Voltare stopped the wheel and undid the straps. Della Marie raised her arms to show that she was unharmed. The crowd clapped and whistled.

The assistant led a beautiful black horse into the arena, and Voltare jumped onto it with one leap.

He immediately stood up on the horse and cantered around the ring, arranging his knives as he went. Urging the horse to go faster, he threw his first knife as they rode past the board. It hit the bull's eye. Round and round they cantered, faster and faster, and each time he passed the board, he threw another knife. Each time, he hit the bull's eye.

Voltare reined in his horse and gracefully slipped off its back. He and Della Marie took their bows to thunderous applause.

"I'm glad that wasn't me up there," said Penny. "Those knives whistled by so close to Della Marie's ears, it's a wonder he didn't cut them off."

"Yeah!" Zinger agreed. "She sure was brave!"

"I think she was crazy to take a chance like that," said Jillybean. "Look at Mandy! She still has her hands in front of her face."

"Dinty, I thought you said that grownups couldn't see you," Penny said. "Then how can Voltare see you?"

"Voltare can see me because he believes in magic. Most circus people believe in magic. But grownups can only see me if I want them to."

The clowns and trick riders filed in again between acts while the crew arranged the set for the next performers. They scampered off as quickly as they came on.

"And now, ladies and gentlemen," Mr. Ferguson's voice boomed over the crowd, "allow me to introduce Andre and his pet seals!"

Andre ran out into the ring followed by three seals. They waddled on flippers and covered the ground very fast. When they caught up with Andre, the seals looked up at him like puppies. They were so adorable. A portable pool had been set up in the center of the ring with steps and a slide. When Andre gave a command, the first seal ran up the steps and slid down the slide, grabbing a huge inflated ball with its flippers as it hit the water.

The other seals followed the first, and with a splash they all landed in the pool. They started to toss the ball to one another, each one catching it on the tip of its nose. This was fun for a while, but then Andre gave one of them another command: the seal flipped the ball onto its nose and started spinning it. The others got in on the act too. While one was spinning the ball, the others clapped their flippers together as though they were applauding. The children thought it was great fun and they laughed with glee.

Andre pointed at a seal with a baton and made a circle in the air. The seal flipped over and over like it was doing cartwheels. Soon, he had all three of them cartwheeling around the pool. Then they all stopped and applauded. The children were delighted.

When Andre threw two more balls into the pool, they each got one and tossed the balls to their right, landing it on the other seals' noses. They passed the balls like this faster and faster until Andre signalled for them to stop. They stopped immediately, and at Andre's command they somersaulted out of the pool and stood upright side by side. They all bowed at the same time as Andre. Then they clapped, of course, honking happily and enjoying the fun. Another bow and they were gone.

"Wasn't that great, Wolfie?" Zinger asked his friend.

"Sure was! Wish we had seals in the river," Wolf said. "You can't play with a fish."

The grownups laughed at the idea of Wolf playing with a fish and joked with him about it.

"If you ever see the fish doing cartwheels and tossing a ball, Wolf," Stormy said with a laugh, "we'll put on a show."

"You can laugh all you like," Zinger grumbled. "But those seals are as smart as dogs."

The pool and the set were removed so that Mr. Ferguson could introduce the next act. "Ladies and gentlemen, meet Darby Muldoon and his entertaining dogs."

Darby Muldoon was dressed in a black top hat and green vest with black pantaloons. He had beet-red chubby cheeks, a wide grin, and a handlebar moustache—and he was followed by a dozen or so dogs of different breeds, colours, and sizes. They trotted alongside him into the ring like they were his children.

"Well, can you beat that?" said Dinty. "It's Darby Muldoon! I didn't know he was still in the circus."

"You know him too?" Penny's eyes opened wide with surprise.

"Sure do! I knew him when he was a young feller. He'd just come over from old Erin and I was hungering for some news about the homeland. So we kind of hit it off. I'll be lookin' forward to seein' him again."

Penny was bewildered. "But he is an old man and you're not old. How could you know him when he was young?"

"Well now, Penny lass," Dinty said. "Leprechauns live to a ripe old age, sometimes six or seven hundred years. I'm still a young feller. I'm only a wee bit over two hundred and fifty."

"Two hundred and fifty years old?" Penny was shocked. "How old are your children?"

"Well now, they were born before trains and airplanes," Dinty told her. "They have a lot of growing up to do! Just watch old Darby. His dogs are really smart."

Darby was leading his dogs through a variety of tricks, jumping through hoops and over hurdles. Then the band started playing a jig and the dogs danced on two feet. A tiny little Chihuahua with large pointed ears danced around all the other dogs, hopping over them one after another so fast that she was like a Mexican jumping bean. Mr. Ferguson said her name was Tricksie. All of the children loved Tricksie and cheered when a big dog tried to catch her and couldn't.

As Darby Muldoon took his bows, the dogs all bowed too.

Dinty nudged Penny. "I'll be back in a few minutes, Penny m'lass. I just want to let old Darby know I'm here. I'll be paying him a visit."

With a whoosh, he was gone.

Penny watched Darby Muldoon as he left the arena. He held out his arm and Penny knew he was carrying Dinty. The old man's face lit up like a Christmas tree. He was so happy to see the friendly elf.

Dinty didn't return until the show was over. He missed the closing cavalcade, and Penny had thought he wasn't coming back. Tommy came over to say goodbye and told them he would see them the next morning. He had another show to do in the evening.

Penny would be celebrating her ninth birthday the next day, so she invited Tommy to come for lemonade and cake at five o'clock.

"Five o'clock is great!" he told her. "The first show is over at four-thirty and the second show doesn't start until seven-thirty."

"Bring Jason and Jenny too, if they would like to come," Penny said. "I'll send Barney to meet you."

"Thanks a lot," Tommy said. "By the way, Jenny is my sister. She's eight years old. I'm sure she and Jason would love to come. We are touring so much, we don't have time to make any friends outside the circus. This will be fun. I have some unpacking to do, so I can't do anything today, but I'm free tomorrow afternoon for a couple of hours. And I'll see you tomorrow morning at eight o'clock for the tour. By the way, do you know a little man called Dinty Finnigan?"

"Yes. He's our friend and hero."

"Well, it was Dinty who saved little Mikey today, not me. He told me he's a leprechaun." Tommy didn't seem surprised that a leprechaun had showed up at the circus.

"I'll tell you all about him tomorrow," Penny said.

"Okay! Eight o'clock in the morning then, and don't be late. The animals have a schedule."

"Super!" Penny was bursting with excitement. "This is going to be the best birthday ever!"

Suddenly, with a whoosh, Dinty reappeared.

"I'll be there too," said Dinty. "I'll bring Mrs. Finnigan and the children. They love lemonade and cake and ice cream."

Penny was jumping up and down with excitement. She filled Summer and Jillybean in on the plans before they tried to push their way through the crowd to the door of the tent. Mr. and Mrs. Henry had invited Summer and Wolf and their parents to stay for the weekend, so they could celebrate Penny's ninth birthday. What fun!

"Did you have a birthday party?" Penny asked Summer. After all, Jillybean and Mandy would be nine in another month and Summer had turned nine three weeks ago.

"We had a barbecue for our tribe. It was great! Everyone made something for me or found something special in the river or woods."

"I was at that one too," said Dinty. "Summer and Wolfie knew I was there, but the grownups didn't."

"Yes! Dinty gave me this special crystal," Summer told her. "Mama put it on a chain for me." She showed Penny the shining pendant hanging around her neck.

"Oh, it's beautiful!" Penny whispered in awe.

"Let's get out of here," Jillybean said. "The crowd seems to have thinned out a bit.

"Good idea!" said Penny.

As they stepped out of the tent into the bright sunlight, a scruffy-looking wizened man rudely shoved Penny on purpose, almost knocking her down.

"Out of the way, little Miss Upstart!" he snarled at her. "Think you are a big star now, do you?"

Penny's wide eyes stared back at him in horror. What on earth had she done to make him so angry? Blackie immediately attacked, swooping down on the man's head and scolding him without mercy.

The man let out a scream, and he found himself sitting on the limb of a big oak tree, fifteen feet up in the air. He must have been wondering how he got up there. Dinty was doing what he did best, protecting his little friend, and Blackie was right in the middle of it, beating on the man with his wings and scaring him so much that he was screaming in terror.

"Wh—why did that horrid m—man attack me?" Penny stammered in a hurt and bewildered voice. "I didn't do anything to him."

"I think he was jealous of you!" Barney said.

"I've never seen him before," said Penny. "Why would he be jealous of me? Do any of you know who he is?"

None of the others knew.

"I thought I saw white paint on his forehead," said Jillybean. "It was smeared into his hair."

"Maybe he was one of the clowns," said Summer. "They wear white paint."

The little gnome-like creature had skittered backwards until he was huddled into the fork of the branch. He had both arms wrapped around a stout limb and he looked like he was settling in to stay for a while.

Dinty left him and rejoined his little friends. "I'll find out who that scoundrel is. I'm going back inside to snoop around a bit. Maybe old Darby Muldoon knows him. If he doesn't, I'll talk to Voltare. Let's just leave the rascal to find his own way down. I don't think he'll try to frighten you again. He's much too shaken right now. If he does, he's got Blackie and me to deal with! He can't see me, so he's pretty spooked."

They looked up at the weird little man, warily watching the group of children. His eyes darted back and forth and his face scrunched up in a puzzled frown. He was still whimpering.

"I don't think he'll come down until we leave," said Dinty. "I'm off to see old Darby and some of my other friends, and I'll see you later. In the meantime, stay away from that rascal! He's bad news!"

"We will, Dinty," Penny said. "You can count on it!"

"If he bothers you again, just send Blackie for me and I'll teach him some manners. I won't be far away."

"What about your wife and children?" Penny asked. "Won't they wonder where you are?"

"Oh, they're right here with me," he told them. "They're a wee bit shy, so they are invisible, for now, but they stay pretty close. I always know where they are."

"That's good," said Penny. "What are their names, Dinty?"

"Thomas, Brian, and Shamus! Say hello to Penny and Summer and the other children!"

Three ghostly voices piped up. "Hi, Penny and Summer, and everybody."

"I can't see you," said Penny. "But pleased to meet you. You too, Mrs. Finnigan!"

"Ah, but she's so polite! Isn't she, Dinty? Nice to meet you too, Penny," said Mrs. Finnigan. "And thank you for inviting us to your birthday party. We'll all be there. Won't we, boys?"

"Aye! That we will!" they all answered together.

All this time, Barney's eyes had been wide with astonishment. He had been able to hear the conversation, but the wonder of not being able to see the elves was hard to understand. He finally decided it was some sort of magic. The birthday party was going to be great fun!

"I'll see you later," said Dinty. "And mind what I said. Stay away from that rascal!"

Penny suggested they all go to the park, but suddenly the rain began to fall. Within a couple of minutes, it was pelting down in buckets. A gust of wind nearly blew them off their feet.

"Where did that come from?" Barney exclaimed. "We'd better find some shelter. We're getting soaked."

"Let's make a run for my house," Penny told them. "We're soaked anyway. We can dry off, Mama will make us some popcorn and hot chocolate, and we'll play Chinese checkers."

"That's a great idea!" said Jillybean, and they all agreed. "Okay! Here we go!"

They ran like antelope, screaming and laughing until they got to the Henry family's front door. Blackie had beaten them home and was perched under the eaves. He looked bedraggled and half-drowned, blinking at them and looking for pity. Penny called him down and snuggled his wet little body under her arm before taking him into the house to dry him off. The nasty, miserable little man in the tree was cold, shivering, wet, and forgotten.

Mama got a roaring fire going and dug out some dry clothes. Then, just as Penny had promised, she treated everyone to hot chocolate and popcorn. Barney grumbled a little because Zinger's clothes were too small for him and he had to wear a pair of Penny's long fleece pants and top. He took a little good-natured teasing but was secretly glad that he was warm and dry.

The sky had turned black and the rain didn't let up as the wind howled and moaned and whipped the branches off the trees. The children looked out from the cozy, warm house, glad that they were inside. Garbage bins rolled down the street and the people ran in every direction to find shelter.

Only then did Penny think about the little man in the tree. She told her parents about their run in with him and of Dinty's and Blackie's part in protecting them. Their parents were horrified that any man, no matter how small he was, would attack a small girl.

"Well, if he's still up in the tree, he must be paying for his bad behaviour," said Papa. "This is not a good time to be out for man or beast." He went over to Blackie, who was now snuggled in a lined boot box, stroking his feathers. "Thank you, Blackie, for protecting my little girl."

"Dinty is going to find out who he is. He knows some of the circus people," Penny told him. The expression on her face suddenly changed. "Oh no! I wonder if the big tent will be all right in the storm."

"I'm sure it will," Papa told them. "The steel guywires and pegs will make it as strong as most houses."

CHAPTER 5

GET ME OUT OF HERE

At seven-thirty sharp on Sunday morning, the kids all met at Penny's house. Mama warned Penny and Zinger that it was Sunday and not to forget to be at Sunday school by eleven o'clock, as they were auditioning children for the Thanksgiving play.

"We won't forget, Mama," Penny promised, "and we'll bring Summer and Wolf with us."

"Good! All right then, I'll see you at the church."

Penny and her friends, including Blackie, arrived at the circus grounds a little early, but Tommy, Jenny, and young Jason were already waiting for them.

"Hi, Penny! Hi, guys!" Tommy greeted them. Gypsy the monkey was perched on his shoulders. "This is my little sister Jenny. And this is Jason."

"Hi, Tommy! Hi, Jenny and Jason!" Penny said, and then she introduced each of her friends. She stroked Blackie's feathers. "And this is Blackie. Blackie, say hi to Tommy!"

"Blackie, say hi to Tommy," Blackie mimicked.

"Cool!" said Tommy delightedly as he tickled Blackie's neck.

Blackie answered by saying "Cool" over and over again until Penny clicked at him twice with her tongue, warning him to be quiet.

"What about Wolfie and me, Penny?" Zinger said in a loud, plaintive whisper. "You forgot about us!"

"Oh yes. This is Wolf and my brother Zinger," Penny said. "Stay real close, boys, and don't get lost!"

"We're not babies!" Zinger complained. "You don't need to worry about us."

"I'll stay with Zinger and Wolf," Jenny promised.

"Good!" said Tommy. "Jenny won't let them get into trouble. She knows her way around the animals. Okay, guys. Let's start at the monkey house."

The monkey house was a long, enclosed trailer on wheels with bars along one side that were covered with fine wire netting. It was set up like a mini-jungle. In one corner was a little cave, surrounded by trees and foliage. Nearby was a family of monkeys, eight in all, a mama and papa and six young ones of various sizes. An attendant dished out breakfast as the monkeys jostled each other to get at the food. Gypsy screeched "Hello," but food was all that was on their tiny minds.

"Did the animals get wet last night?" Zinger asked.

"No. There are sliding doors to protect them from the weather," Tommy told them. "The monkeys sleep in the cave and they are very comfortable in there. The attendants brush them down and keep them clean. We also clean the trailers every day."

"I want to see the lions," said Zinger.

"Okay, Zinger. That happens to be next on the tour. Just follow me!"

Tommy led the little group to another large trailer on wheels. It was similar to the monkey house but was divided into two separate rooms with bars all around, like a cage.

"Why does it have two rooms?" Barney asked.

"That's so we can lock down one side when the attendants go in to clean the cage and set out the meals. The divider is operated from the outside so that when the cage is ready, the divider is raised and the lions move from one side to the other. Then the divider is lowered and the attendant can go into the other side and clean that cage and leave water without fear of being attacked. The only people who dare to be in the cage with the lions are my mother and my brother Martin. Mom brushes them and curries their manes. They like the attention, but I wouldn't want to try it."

"Your mama and brother are very brave," said Penny. "Oh look! A man is going into the cage now!"

"Yes! The pride is all gathered in one cage. Watch how fast the attendant hoses the cage down, dries it out, and covers it with fresh straw. Then he sets up the food. He's very careful not to get water on the cats. They hate water."

"Where do you keep the elephants?" Summer asked. "They are so huge, they wouldn't have much room in a trailer."

"They have a tent and their own corral. The tent protects them from the weather and the corral gives them room to move around. Because of their size, they are the most difficult to transport. Follow me and I'll show you."

Suddenly, they heard a loud wail.

"Get me out of here!" Zinger howled. He had sneaked into the cage when the attendant was feeding the lions, and now hid behind a box. With the attendant gone, Zinger became hysterical. The attendant had left the centre divider up to give the lions space to move around after they had finished feeding.

"Oh no!" Tommy cried in alarm. "I don't think I can lift the lever. It's very heavy."

"Maybe we can lift it together," Jason suggested.

"Good idea!" said Tommy. "Start climbing, Jason! And somebody had better go get Martin!"

Just then, some men from the crew arrived.

"I'll get him," one of them said, and he was off like a rocket.

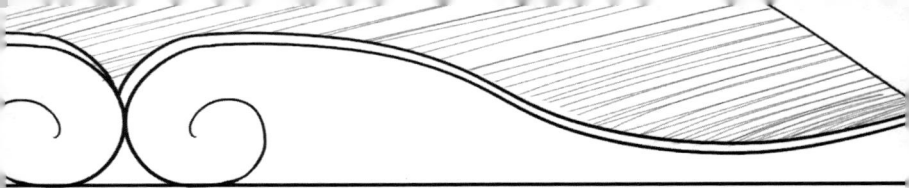

"Not to fear! Dinty's here!" shouted a disembodied voice. "Don't be frightened, Zinger m'lad. Just be quiet and do what I tell you."

"Okay, Dinty!" Zinger was scared to death and he was sniffling, but with his hero here, he suddenly realized there was hope. He might not die, after all.

Simba stopped eating and began to slink across the cage to see what was going on. His tail swished back and forth, angry that this little human had disturbed his breakfast. Zinger scrunched back as far as he could against the wall and stared in horror at the big cat. Then, like a miracle, Dinty allowed the children to see him as he took a flying leap through the bars and onto the lion's head.

"I'm going to talk to Simba here," Dinty told Zinger.

Tommy and Jason had reached the lever just as Dinty started to hold a conversation with the startled cat. Penny tried to keep Zinger's attention off Simba by talking quietly to him and reminding him that Dinty would never let anything happen to him. The other lions were still eating and paid very little attention to what was going on, but Zinger was whimpering and shaking so much that Penny was afraid he would alert the others.

Dinty whispered into Simba's ear and the lion angrily tried to shake him off his head. Simba swatted at Dinty a couple of times without success.

Suddenly, the big cat stood still and listened to what Dinty was telling him in animal language. He then turned and went to join the other lions. A small crowd of circus people gathered and called encouragement to Zinger, and also to Tommy and Jason.

"It's just like Daniel in the lions' den," one man said in a husky voice. "The lions aren't going near him."

They couldn't see Dinty, and it looked like a miracle to everyone but the children. By now, Tommy and Jason had managed to pry the lever up and the divider slammed down, just as Martin arrived, to a cry of relief from the watchers.

"Okay, Zinger," Dinty said. "Let's get out of here."

Tommy and Martin were already at the door when Martin lifted the bar to let them out.

Penny grabbed Zinger in a bear hug and almost crushed him to death. "I really should be mad at you, Zinger, but I'm so glad you're all right. I'm usually the one who gets into trouble, so I can't be too mad at you. How on earth did you get in the cage in the first place?"

"I just lifted the bar and walked in. I thought the lions were in the other room. When I saw that the room wasn't divided, I tried to get out, but the bar had fallen down. It only opens from the outside and I was trapped. I was so scared, Penny." Zinger's lip trembled.

"Those doors are supposed to be locked," Tommy told them. "I'm going to report this to my dad. There's no way Zinger should have been able to get in there. I'm sorry, Penny and Zinger."

Just then, Wolf and Jenny appeared.

"Where did you go, Zinger?" Jenny asked. "You were supposed to stay with us! We've been looking for you."

"I'm sorry, Jenny. I wanted to see the lions." Zinger hung his head in shame. "I wish I'd stayed with you."

"Don't worry," said Martin. "Somebody's going to pay for this negligence. I will track the culprit down."

Penny glared at her brother. "Zinger is the one who should be sorry. Now, maybe you'll listen and stay with the rest of us. Otherwise, I'll take you home right now. You could have been Simba's breakfast."

An expression of horror came over Zinger's face as his mind conjured up an image of the lion's dinner, with himself as the main course. "I promise I'll stay real close to you, Penny," he whispered.

Nobody noticed the nasty little man who had attacked Penny the previous day. He slinked furtively away towards the elephant corral with a fiendishly ugly grimace on his face.

"Do you still feel like going to see the elephants?" Tommy asked. "Do you think Zinger is okay?"

"He's okay! And he's promised to be good," said Penny. "How about the rest of you? Do you still want to finish the tour?"

"Oh yes!" they all shouted. "Let's go!"

They spent the next couple of hours visiting the elephants, seals, bears, Darby Muldoon's dogs, and the beautiful Arabian horses, among many other animals. The performers were very kind to them. Penny was hoping to see Mahmoud to thank him for helping her when she had performed in the show, but he wasn't in the elephants' corral. Tommy tried to locate him but didn't have any luck.

The clowns made a fuss over Penny and her friends, and Mr. Ferguson and his wife Lynda welcomed them as though they had known them for years. Jenny stuck like glue to Zinger and Wolf to keep them out of trouble. She blamed herself for not keeping a better eye on Zinger. And Jason and Tommy were perfect hosts.

The time went by far too quickly and soon Penny and her friends had to leave for Sunday school.

"Don't forget my birthday party!" Penny said.

"We won't, Penny," Tommy assured her. "We'll be there! Save us some cake and ice cream!"

They made it to Sunday school just in time, but Miss Sprightly and Mrs. Beasley, the vicar's wife, found it almost impossible to keep order in the class now that there was a circus performer in their midst. At last, Mrs. Beasley asked Penny to come up to the front of the class to tell them about her short experience as a performer and how it had come about.

Thankfully, the class settled down and Penny got her chance to be the star. When she was finished talking, she invited all the other children to her birthday party. Mrs. Beasley knew for sure who she wanted to play the lead in the Thanksgiving play. Penny got the part without having to audition.

CHAPTER 6

HAPPY BiRTHDAY, PENNY

Papa and Stormy set up a huge gazebo-style tent in the backyard, and Autumn and Mama decorated it with balloons and prepared a long table loaded with cakes, pies, and lemonade. As the children arrived in droves, Mama hoped there would be enough for everyone. She hadn't expected so many. When she heard that Penny had invited her whole Sunday school class, she was no longer surprised.

"I wish you had told me you were going to invite the whole class, Penny," she said, scolding her impulsive daughter. "Thank goodness I went to the bakery yesterday, just in case."

"Don't worry, Mama! There is enough here to feed half the town," Penny said. "I've sent Barney to fetch Tommy and Jason and Jenny. They'll be here any minute. I wonder if Dinty is here with his family yet?"

"Right here! Front and centre, Penny m'lass!" Dinty said. "The missus and I and the children will find a spot in the trees where we won't get stepped on."

"Help yourself to anything you want off the table, and don't be shy," Penny told them.

Just then, they heard a loud commotion as Tommy, Jason, and Jenny arrived on beautiful white ponies. Barney was panting and gasping for breath from racing along beside them. Gypsy was perched on Tommy's shoulders, grinning and clapping his hands with glee.

"Ponies!" Penny yelled excitedly. "Everybody, listen! They're here!"

Tommy and his friends dismounted.

"You can't have a party without pony rides," Tommy said, grinning with delight. "I hope the kids have fun riding!"

"Thank goodness we have a big back acreage," Papa murmured.

Penny clapped her hands with glee. "Pony rides! Oh, this is going to be the best party!"

She introduced Tommy, Jason, and Jenny to all the other kids, and everybody wanted to ride the ponies.

"Don't worry," Tommy assured them. "You'll all get a turn!"

Miss Sprightly had made up a list of games for the kids to play—three blind mice, a three-legged race, a fifty-yard dash—with prizes for those who came in first, second, and third. While some were riding, others played games. They were each given three minutes on the ponies. It was hard to keep track sometimes, as they didn't want to get off.

It was indeed a wonderful party.

"Help yourselves when you want to eat," Mama shouted to get their attention. "Mrs. Beasley and I will dish out the ice cream. Just bring your plate over here!"

There was a mad dash for the food and lemonade.

Many of the kids had brought presents for Penny, and she started opening them to squeals of delight as she discovered everything she really wanted.

Tommy, Jason, and Jenny came to stand in front of her with wide grins on their faces.

"We have something to tell you, Penny," Tommy said. "Jason, Jenny, and I just want you to know that this is the very first party we've ever been invited to by someone outside the circus. And we've never had so much fun. So we would like to give you a present to remember us by. Jenny, bring Swallow over here."

Jenny led the little pony over and handed the reins to Penny.

"Swallow is our present to you, Penny, from the three of us. She's yours now. She is very gentle and I know you

will take very good care of her." He handed her a paper with instructions. "This is what she eats, and you have lots of grass here with plenty of room for her. You even have a shed for when she needs to get in out of the weather. We would also like you to have another twelve tickets for this evening's show."

Penny's eyes were filled with tears of joy. "Oh, I must be dreaming," she whispered. "This is too perfect! You really want to give me this beautiful pony? You mean, she's really mine? Forever?"

"Yes! We'll have to leave in about twenty minutes. Some of the kids haven't had a chance to ride, so now they can come back tomorrow and have their three minutes like everybody else."

"Oh, thank you, thank you, thank you!" Penny gushed, and she gave Tommy, Jenny, and Jason hugs all around. "If you are ever in Green Oaks again, you must come and see us, and we could write to each other and always be friends. I'll tell you how Swallow is doing, so you won't miss her so much."

"That's right," said Mama. "And our door is always open to you and your families."

"Thank you!" Tommy said. "We'll remember that! Now, we'd better have our cake and ice cream before we go."

"All you can eat, my boy! All you can eat," said Papa. "Well, Penny, my dear, you've got a responsibility now. You will have to feed Swallow on time, make sure she has water, and brush her every day."

Penny's face was glowing. "And I will ride her every day so she gets enough exercise."

"She's beautiful!" Summer whispered as she stroked the lovely white coat. "I wish she was mine."

"You can ride her anytime, Summer," Penny assured her friend. "Jillybean and Mandy too."

"Boy, Penny, you sure have all the luck," Barney grumbled. "There must be an angel following you around. Nothing like that ever happens to me."

"Yes it does, Barney," Penny pointed out. "You're going to the show again tonight, for free."

"Oh yeah!" Barney's face brightened up. "I forgot about that. Thanks, Penny!"

Suddenly, Dinty and his family appeared next to Penny's little group. Tommy, Jason, and Jenny's eyes lit up, because they could see the leprechauns too.

"You're a grand group of kids," Dinty said.

"Thanks, Dinty," said Tommy. "And thank you for helping little Mikey yesterday."

"I'm always there in a pinch," said Dinty.

"Well, we have to go," Jason reminded Tommy. "Don't forget, my act is up first."

Tommy nodded. "That's right! Okay, everybody, we'll see you later. Don't be late!"

They hugged Penny and wished her a happy birthday again, and then they were gone.

"I've got a present for you, Penny, from the Finnigans," Dinty told her. "It's a special crystal. If you talk into it, I will hear you. If you're in trouble and need help, just talk into it and say, 'Penny calling Dinty!'"

"It's like having my own telephone," Penny said. "And it has a beautiful chain, so I can wear it around my neck all the time. Thanks again, Dinty! Okay, everybody, we'd better get going, or we'll be late. We've got front row seats again!"

CHAPTER 7

SKULDUGGERY

Mama had the job of telling everyone that the party was over. Nobody wanted to leave, but by ten minutes after seven, the last child had gone. Barney had left fifteen minutes ago with tickets for his parents, as they had been unable to go to the show the previous afternoon. Penny distributed the rest of the tickets to her friends and their families.

They managed to make it to the circus just five minutes before curtain and were in their seats when the horns trumpeted the start of the show. It was thrilling to see a repeat of the show and watch their friends fly around the arena.

Suddenly, Dinty claimed Penny's armrest and whispered to her. "Something is wrong! Mahmoud is missing and they'll have to put in a substitute."

"Oh no!" Penny kept her voice low. "I wonder what has happened to him. He wasn't around this morning, either. Do they have any idea where he could be?"

"No! But I'm going back to snoop around. Don't worry. They can't see me, so I'm the perfect snoop. See you later!"

And with a whoosh, he was gone.

Dinty flitted around the performers and checked out the animals. When he dropped in on the elephants, he noticed there was a new elephant trainer all dressed up in the satin costume Mahmoud had worn. There was something familiar about him, and Dinty darted over to get a closer look. It was the nasty little man who had attacked Penny.

Dinty went in search of Tommy before confronting the scoundrel. He found Tommy getting ready to ride between acts. Dinty jumped up onto the horse.

"Greetings, Tommy, m'lad," Dinty said. "I've some bad news for you!"

"Dinty? Is that you?"

"Indeed it is. I just thought you should know that your new elephant trainer is the miserable scamp who attacked Penny yesterday. I wondered if he might be responsible for Mahmoud's disappearance. He's more than ready to step into Mahmoud's job."

"Thanks, Dinty. I'll tell Martin when I'm finished this round. Martin will check him out!"

Tommy was off like a shot, following Jason around the arena.

As soon as the riders were back, Tommy told Martin about the substitute elephant trainer and how he'd attacked Penny the previous day. He also revealed Dinty's suspicions that the man might be responsible for Mahmoud's disappearance.

Martin decided to go in search of the scoundrel. "Tommy, go ask Jason to suit up and fill in for Mahmoud. The rest of you men from the crew, get a search party going to find Mahmoud."

Martin found the rascal in the elephants' corral. He was already dressed in Mahmoud's costume and was getting ready to lead the elephants to the big top.

"Who told you to take Mahmoud's place in the show?" Martin asked. "You're only a helper!"

"Well, sir, when Mahmoud didn't show up, I knew you'd need me," the man said.

"You were wrong. We don't need you. Jason is filling in for Mahmoud. Now, get out of those clothes immediately!"

"But I have experience! I've been working with the elephants and they know me."

"They know Jason also," Martin answered, "and you are not an acrobat. I don't have time now to discuss this, but I want to see you in my father's trailer after the show."

"Yes, sir," the man grunted.

Jason showed up at that moment. He had changed into a red satin costume. "Will this do, Martin? I need a long scarf for a turban!"

"You look great, Jason! Look through Mahmoud's trunk. There will be something there you can use."

"Okay."

"You know the routine, so you'll be fine!" Martin told him.

The little man squeaked like a rat and ran as fast as his short legs would carry him through the tent flap and out into the night.

"Well, that got rid of him," Martin said.

Dinty called on his old friend Darby and requested the use of one of the dog-trainer's large hounds. Dinty took one of Mahmoud's coats off the rack in the corral, and the dog took a good whiff. He was off like a shot, sniffing and snuffling. Dinty rode him like a horse, hanging onto the dog's collar like a rodeo contestant.

Martin dialled 911. "Hello! This is Martin Ferguson from the Ferguson Family Circus. One of our star performers is missing. Would you please send a man around to the back entrance of the big top, and ask for Martin? I think foul play might be involved."

When Jason found Mahmoud's trunk, Darby's dog was standing to attention and pointing at the trunk with its tail ramrod straight.

"Hold it, Jason!" Dinty appeared before Jason. "I think you'd better get Martin or one of the other men to open this trunk. I have a feeling you're about to find your elephant trainer."

Jason called Martin to come quickly, and Martin came running at a gallop into the tent. The dog hadn't moved a muscle and was still pointing.

"What is it, Jason?" Martin asked impatiently. "Stop fooling around and get moving! You should be ready! You're on after the next act!"

Jason just pointed to the trunk. "I think you'd better open the trunk, Martin. Misty is pretty excited."

"Oh, for goodness sake!" Martin grabbed the hasp and yanked it off. He raised the lid and stared into the terrified eyes of Mahmoud. The elephant trainer was trussed up like a chicken and had blood running down his face from a deep cut. His mouth had been taped up and he seemed in very bad shape.

"Mahmoud!" Jason and Martin echoed together.

Just then, a detective arrived from the police station, asking for Martin. He gave the situation the once-over; it didn't take him long to realize the truth of the matter.

"Well, I take it this is your missing performer," he observed.

"Yes! Get him out of there!" Martin ordered the crew. "Be gentle now! Danny, go find Doctor Teegan."

The men lifted poor little Mahmoud out of the trunk and placed him carefully on the table. He was whimpering and shaking as they peeled the tape and ropes off him. He had no feeling in his arms and legs. The ropes had been tied so tightly that the circulation was cut off.

As soon as the ropes were removed, he tried to get up and couldn't manage it. He was very agitated.

"I must get ready for my show!" Mahmoud cried.

"This is going to require stitches," the doctor said. "And he's lost a lot of blood. He's not working tonight."

"You heard the doctor, Mahmoud." Martin tried to soothe him by speaking softly. "Jason is filling in for you. Now get going, Jason! Grab a scarf and go!"

Jason did as he was told and scampered off.

"Who did this to you, Mahmoud?" Martin asked.

"Drobo, the helper."

"Why did he hurt you?" the detective inquired.

"He want my job!" Mahmoud said in imperfect English. "I see him this morning open lion cage. I thought he help clean cage, but then little boy go into cage and Drobo drop bar. He see me watch him, and when I ran to open cage to let little boy out, Drobo hit me over head with spade. That all I remember. Oh, Mr. Martin, please tell me I won't lose job because I can't do show tonight. It not my fault. Drobo bad man!"

"Don't worry, Mahmoud," Martin said. "Your job is safe, but we'll have to find a new helper for you. Drobo is going to jail. We don't need troublemakers in the circus."

The show proceeded as usual while all this skulduggery was being exposed backstage. Jason led the elephants out and performed Mahmoud's act without a single mistake.

When it was Tommy's turn, Mr. Ferguson asked Penny to join him again as his partner. This time she wasn't nervous, and as Tommy led her out onto the floor, the band played "Happy Birthday."

"This is Penny's birthday, ladies and gentlemen," Mr. Ferguson's voice boomed over the loud speaker. "Come on, children, let's hear you sing and wish her a happy birthday."

The crowd all joined in.

When Tommy and Penny were in their saddles, Penny felt as though she was on top of the world. Jason did a wonderful job. The elephants were used to him, because he always worked with Tommy and Mahmoud. It turned out they usually didn't ask someone to join them from the audience, but they had wanted to say thank you to Penny for finding Gypsy.

Dinty tracked the evil little villain with the help of Darby's dog, Misty. They found one of Drobo's shirts hanging on a nail, and one whiff was all Misty needed. She discovered Drobo cowering under one of the trailers.

Dinty decided to have some fun with him.

Misty stood over Drobo with her legs splayed out so she was almost on her stomach. Her tail pointed straight up.

"Thought you could get away from me, did you?" Dinty asked.

From Drobo's perspective, the voice seemed to be coming from the dog. He groaned with dread.

"Go away!" Drobo whined. "Dogs can't talk. Please go away!"

"No! I'm going to stay right here until they come for you. I'm going to watch while they take you away to jail. It's what you deserve. Don't move now!"

Drobo cringed, trying to make himself even smaller than he already was. "I won't move. Please don't hurt me!"

Misty's tongue was hanging out and she was slobbering like a tap.

Dinty decided this was a good time to fetch some help. He darted off to find Tommy.

By the time Dinty found him, Jason and Tommy had finished their act.

"Ah, there you are," Dinty said. "I just wanted to let you know that Misty has Drobo cornered."

Martin and the detective were then informed of the proceedings.

"Follow me!" said Dinty, and he led them all to the trailer.

Only Tommy could see Dinty. Misty was still standing guard, her four legs spread north, south, east, and west. She looked so funny that Martin had to laugh.

"Good girl, Misty!" Martin said. "To heel now!"

They all heard a sigh of relief come from under the trailer.

"All right, Drobo, out you come, or I'll send Misty in there to get you," Martin threatened.

Drobo screamed in terror. "No, no! Don't do that! I'll come out. Don't let that devil dog come near me!"

"Devil dog?" they all echoed in disbelief.

Martin and the kids roared with laughter, because Misty was one of the most gentle, well-behaved dogs in the world. She would lick a person to death rather than attack. Drobo slithered out on his stomach, just like the snake he was. The detective then read him his rights and snapped the handcuffs on his wrists.

"Come with me, Mr. Trouble!" the detective said. "We have a nice cage waiting, just for you. You'll be joining my circus now."

With that, the detective led him to the police van.

Martin and the boys hurried back to the show. Martin's act had been rescheduled because of all the trouble. It would be the last feature before intermission. In spite of all the backstage intrigue, the show had proceeded without any interruption.

When intermission was announced, they each gave a sigh of relief. There would be a short rest and then they'd have to get to work again.

Dinty joined his friends and family and brought everyone up to date on the backstage goings-on.

"Thank goodness they caught him," Penny said. "Poor Mahmoud! And imagine that man doing such a thing to my little brother. I hope he'll be in jail for a long time."

"Mahmoud seems to be doing all right," Dinty reported. "The last I saw, all the ladies of the circus wanted to take care of him. I don't think he's had so much attention in his whole life. Anyway, he'll be up and around in a couple of days."

After the show was over, Tommy and Jason took Penny and her friends backstage to see Mahmoud.

"Thank you, Mahmoud," said Zinger, "for trying to save my life."

"And I'm so sorry you got hurt," Penny said.

Mahmoud's face beamed at being treated like a hero.

"Mahmoud happy little brother okay, Missy," Mahmood said. "It be bad thing if Simba get little brother!"

Mr. Ferguson came backstage, smiling. "Well, well, well! If it isn't our newest little star, Penny Henry. You did a grand job out there. I might hire you some day."

"Thank you, sir," said Penny. "It was fun!"

"Tommy and Jenny haven't stopped talking about you. I think you will all be grand friends," the ringmaster said. "Too bad we're on the road so much. But you can always keep in touch by writing. Here's my card! This address and mobile telephone number will always help you find us."

"Oh, thank you, Mr. Ferguson." Penny placed the card in her pocket and determined she would put it in her case when she got home so it wouldn't get lost.

All the kids were sad as they said goodbye to their new friends.

"We'll be on the circuit for the next eight months," Tommy told Penny. "Then we take two months of holidays. But remember to write, and I'll phone every now and then. And don't forget, we'll be back next year."

"I'll never forget any of you," Penny said, and she knew she wouldn't. "We'll be friends for life. And I'll take real good care of Swallow. She is the most wonderful present I've ever had in my whole life. You'll just have to come visit her on holidays. And every time I ride her, I will think of you."

Mama and Papa and the other parents were waiting by the big top entrance for them.

"I suppose none of you will sleep tonight," Papa chuckled. "What an exciting couple of days you have had."

Penny grinned. "I can just imagine what school will be like tomorrow."

Barney groaned. He knew one thing for certain: sticking with Penny for the last two days was the smartest thing he had ever done.

CHAPTER 8

SWEET DREAMS

When Penny went to sleep that night, she dreamed she was flying like the wind around the circus arena on Swallow's back, alongside Tommy and Jason. They were the stars, and the crowd was clapping and cheering them on. Barney was the ringmaster and Jillybean and Zinger were lion tamers. She thought this was very funny.

When she woke up, she remembered the dream, and she laughed so hard that she woke up the rest of the family. They weren't amused, because it was only six-thirty.

Penny hurried into her clothes and ran out of the house to check on Swallow. The little pony was glad to see her. When Penny gave her a lump of sugar, Swallow snuggled her nose against Penny's face.

"I love you, Swallow," Penny whispered softly. "And I'll take real good care of you. Papa is going to get some oats today, and there's plenty of grass here for you until then."

She brushed Swallow with long, loving strokes of her own hairbrush.

"We'll get you your own hairbrush today. It was so sweet of Tommy to give me the saddle as well. I hope you don't mind if some of the kids come over to get a ride, since they missed out at the birthday party."

Papa had been standing in the doorway for the past couple of minutes, listening to Penny's sweet talk to her pony. He smiled as he watched her, and knew she would take real good care of Swallow.

"Well, I caught you talking to the pony, didn't I?" Papa chuckled. "Poor old Tumbleweed will be taking a back seat from now on."

"I've been thinking, Papa. Why don't we fix up the shed?" Penny suggested "There's room for both Tumbleweed and Swallow in there. We can turn it into a nice, comfortable stable. Tumbleweed's getting old, and we don't have to keep her at the shop. They would be company for each other. Swallow's used to being around other horses, and she might be lonely all by herself."

"What a good idea! I was thinking of doing something like that for Tumbleweed. She's almost getting too old to pull the cart anymore, except for short runs. Besides, the old truck is still in pretty good shape for hauling scrap."

Penny gave him a big hug. "Oh, thank you, Papa! You're the best papa in the world."

"Well, thank you, my dear. But I'd better get moving if I'm going to pick up some oats from Tumbleweed's shed and bring her back here before business starts for the day."

"And don't forget to bring a curry brush as well," Penny suggested.

Papa smiled to himself, enjoying the fact his young daughter had taken on a new sense of responsibility.

"Penny!" Mama stuck her head out of the window. "Penny! There's a phone call for you from Tommy!"

Penny almost ran over her mama to get to the phone.

"Hi, Tommy! You're up early," she said.

"We're packed and ready to leave," he told her. "We just wanted to say goodbye again and thank you for everything. How's Swallow?"

"I brushed her this morning and gave her sugar. Papa is going to bring oats for her this morning. I dreamed about her all night." Penny was rambling on and on.

"That's great! Well, Jenny and Jason are here and want to say goodbye. Hold on!"

Jason and Jenny took turns on the phone saying their goodbyes, and then Tommy came back on.

"I suppose you have to get ready for school," he said.

"Yes! Don't you go to school, Tommy?"

"We have a tutor who travels with us. We have school, just like you, except that it's set around the circus schedule.

While we're travelling, we spend lots of time studying. We have to go now, Penny. I promise to write and phone you."

"Bye, Tommy! And thanks a hundred times for Swallow. Have a safe trip!"

•

Blackie perched on Penny's shoulder as she rode her bike to school. Penny chattered excitedly to him all the way, and he chattered right back. She was still highly excited when she arrived.

She was soon surrounded by students. Everybody wanted to be her friend, and when Miss Sprightly entered the room, it took some time before she could restore order to the class.

"Well," said Miss Sprightly with a smile, "I see that you have managed to become the centre of attention once again, Penny. I suppose we won't get any work done today until we hear all about it. So why don't you come up to the front and tell us how you managed to become a star in the circus. That's every child's dream. I do hope you're writing everything in a journal, because I don't know any other girl who has the adventures you do."

Penny went up to the front and held everyone spellbound, including Miss Sprightly, for almost an hour. She ended by telling them all about Swallow and how she wished she could have brought her to school for Show and Tell.

Penny was one of Miss Sprightly's brightest pupils, and the teacher loved to hear about Penny's adventures—or misadventures, as the case may be. How she wished her childhood had been so full and exciting. So she encouraged Penny's adventurous spirit and lived her lost childhood through Penny.

It was a long day for Penny. She couldn't wait to get home to ride Swallow. Barney and Jillybean rode home with her on their bikes.

Penny couldn't believe it, but when they arrived at her house, about a dozen kids had beaten them home and were waiting in her backyard for their promised rides. Poor Swallow! It took over two hours for all the kids to get their rides.

Barney was pleased as punch when Penny gave him the important job of ringmaster. He decided how long the ride should be for each kid. They were all beat, including Swallow, when the last kid finally left.

Zinger brought out a chair and pretended to be the lion tamer, worrying poor old Frisky to death. For a dog, Frisky usually didn't have a lot of get-up-and-go, so he was pretty upset with Zinger; he growled and knocked over the chair, just like Simba would. Of course, this made the play all the more real to Zinger.

Miss Sprightly dropped over to see Penny's pony, Swallow, and Penny was surprised when the teacher asked if she could have a ride.

"I waited until all the other children were gone, because I didn't want them to see me on the pony at my age," Miss

Sprightly said. "You see, I used to ride when I was a young girl. I've always missed it."

Miss Sprightly rode at a fair canter around the back acreage and surprised everyone. She hadn't needed any help to get on the pony, as lots of the kids had. She just vaulted up like a young girl.

"You can ride her anytime, Miss Sprightly," Penny said. "You sure are a good rider."

"Thank you, Penny. My father used to breed racehorses, and I rode them to give them exercise."

Mama then made hotdogs and lemonade for the would-be circus performers, and hoped things would calm down after a day or two.

As Penny hugged Swallow, and Blackie snuggled up against her cheek for a kiss, she thought about the past weekend and the wonderful friends she had made. She was sure she must be the luckiest girl in the whole wide world. What more could a girl ask for?

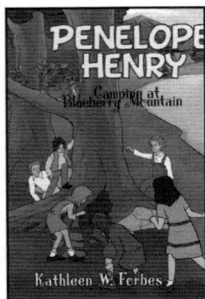

Camping at Blueberry Mountain
978-1-4866-0797-6

An adventure is afoot in the town of Green Oaks as eight-year-old Penelope Henry gets the best surprise of her summer: a camping trip to beautiful Blueberry Mountain. The whole family—including her mama, papa, and brother Zinger—pack up their cart and head into the wilderness to relax, meet new lifelong friends, and learn valuable lessons that will forever change them.

But not everything about Blueberry Mountain is as peaceful as it seems. When a group of bandits start causing trouble in camp, it's up to Penny and her friends to save the day—with the help of an irreverent leprechaun named Dinty, who only appears to children.

NEXT IN THE *PENELOPE HENRY* SERIES:

Country Jamboree
978-1-4866-1000-6

Country Jamboree will take you on a weekend of fun for the whole family. Join Penelope and her family and friends down on the farm for a rodeo with their country cousins where they'll watch the horse racing, the chuck wagons, and trick riding! Encounter mystery and discovery with surprises around every corner. Although facing danger and uncertainty, Penelope and friends are protected by Dinty Finnigan, the Irish leprechaun who protects small children and brings fun and magic everywhere he goes. Penelope and her friends will guide you on adventures great and small as they explore the farm and all the fun to be had!

Also available by Kathleen W. Forbes:

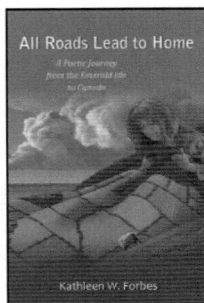

All Roads Lead to Home
978-1-4866-0789-1

Kathleen has discovered something magical in every province of this grand country, Canada. She sees the beauty in God's gifts to us: the mountains, the valleys, the trees, and the rivers and lakes, which have all inspired her poetry. Most poems are spiritual, some are for children, and some are just plain silly. Come and journey through the hills of Ireland, the cities of Ontario, and the majestic mountains of British Columbia with Kathleen's poetry. She hopes you find something to warm your heart.

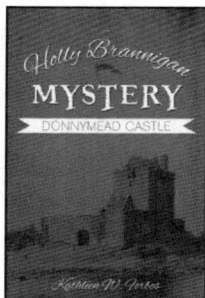

Donnymead Castle
978-1-4866-0801-0

When Holly and her family visit Holly's grandmother in her cottage on the grounds of Donnymead Castle, Holly is fascinated with the castle and manages to talk the caretaker into giving her a tour. But mysterious activity has been taking place on the castle grounds and Holly will have to put her sleuthing skills to the test.

Join Holly and her friend Tim on their explorations of the ancient village. Trace the threads of history from the past into the future and follow Holly and Tim as they discover that things aren't always as they appear. As the mystery deepens, Holly and Tim become lost in history, but can they discover who is behind the criminal activity in Donnymead?

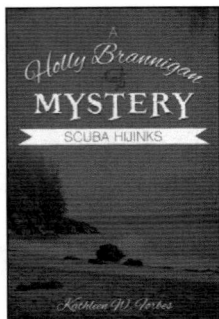

Scuba Hijinks
978-1-4866-0805-8

Scuba Hijinks is the second book in the *Holly Brannigan Mystery* series. Set on the West Coast of Canada in the Lions Bay and Porteau Bay area, the story follows the adventures of teen sleuth Holly Brannigan and her friends, Bonnie, Paul, and Ted as they team up with Holly's father, Detective David Brannigan, to catch a gang of rogue scuba divers. Holly and her friends learn to scuba dive in order to pursue the criminals, and they bravely face challenges and dangers throughout the case. Thrust into a world of kidnapping and vandalism, the amateur detectives use their new skills and unlimited trust in each other to bring the gang to justice.

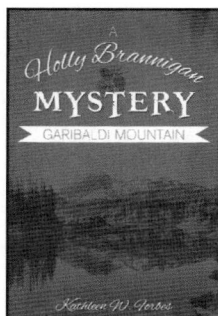

Garibaldi Mountain
978-1-4866-1124-9

Holly Brannigan and her three teenage friends—Paul Castles, Ted Lumley, and her best friend, Bonnie Tilson—have helped attorney David Brannigan, Holly's father, on cases in the past, but this is the most dangerous mystery yet. A family with three children has disappeared, along with a close friend of the family, while camping in Garibaldi Provincial Park. When Holly and her friends hear of the disaster, they join a Mountain Search and Rescue team of volunteers to help the search. In very short order, Holly's team find clues that make them suspicious of foul play.

Follow Holly and her team as they search through torrential rain and fog, confront a dangerous wolf and its pack, and dodge men with bows and arrows who are terrorizing them as they race the clock to find the missing family. There are new threats and dangers at every turn!

A Holly Brannigan Mystery: Garibaldi Mountain is the third in the series.